Nazar

Author:
Tom Ratliff studied American history at Central Connecticut State University and the University of Connecticut. He teaches US history and world civilisation at Central Connecticut State University, and has authored several books for young readers. This is his seventh book for The Salariya Book Company.

Artist:
Mark Bergin was born in Hastings, England, in 1961. He studied at Eastbourne College of Art and specialises in historical reconstructions, aviation and maritime subjects. He lives in Bexhill-on-Sea, England, with his wife and children.

Series creator:
David Salariya was born in Dundee, Scotland. He has illustrated a wide range of books and has created and designed many new series for publishers in the UK and overseas. David established The Salariya Book Company in 1989. He lives in Brighton, England, with his wife, illustrator Shirley Willis, and their son, Jonathan.

Editor: Stephen Haynes

Editorial Assistant: Mark Williams

Published in Great Britain in MMXII by
Book House, an imprint of
The Salariya Book Company Ltd
25 Marlborough Place, Brighton BN1 1UB
www.salariya.com
www.book-house.co.uk

HB ISBN-13: 978-1-908177-95-7
PB ISBN-13: 978-1-908177-96-4

SALARIYA

1 3 5 7 9 8 6 4 2

A CIP catalogue record for this book is available from the British Library.

Printed and bound in China.

PAPER FROM SUSTAINABLE FORESTS

Avoid being a Pony Express Rider!

Written by
Tom Ratliff

Illustrated by
Mark Bergin

Created and designed by
David Salariya

The Danger Zone™

BOOK HOUSE

Contents

Introduction

You are the 16-year-old son of a pioneer family in Kansas Territory. In the spring of 1860 you read an ad for a direct mail service that will connect the eastern United States with California. The Pony Express will cross 3,164 km (1,966 miles) of prairie, mountains and desert between St Joseph, Missouri, and Sacramento, California, in only 10 days! A relay system will provide fresh horses and riders at regular intervals.

The Express Company will need 80 to 100 riders, and stationmasters to maintain and operate more than 150 stations. Stock handlers will be needed to take care of the horses; 400 to 500 horses are required to keep the riders in the saddle.

Riders are paid $25 a week, which is more than most people earn in a month. So, with the promise of adventure and a chance to earn some money of your own, you decide to try your luck as a rider.

Some say there was a genuine advertisement just like this – but no-one can prove it!

What is the Pony Express?

The Pony Express, or Central Overland California and Pike's Peak Express Company, is owned by the firm of Russell, Majors and Waddell. They have invested $60,000 in the venture in hopes of winning a contract from the US government to deliver mail to California.

Creating a rapid mail-delivery system takes skill, foresight and organisation. The 3,200 km (2,000-mile) route requires relay stations every 8 to 32 km (5 to 20 miles), and many of these have to be built in the mountains, deserts and open prairie. Several hundred horses have to be purchased, and scores of young men interviewed and tested, before the Pony Express is ready for business.

William Russell

Alexander Majors

William Waddell

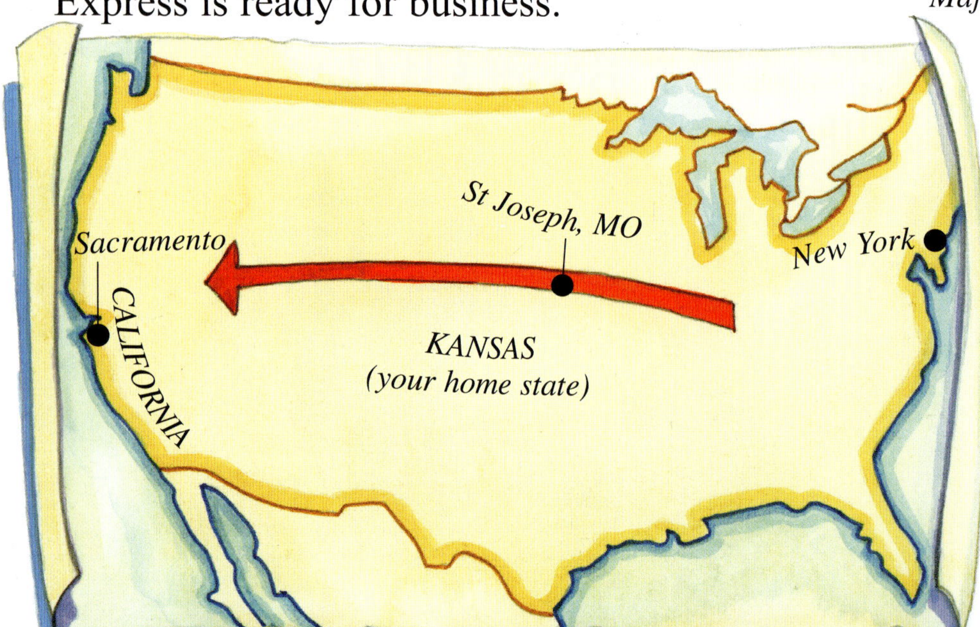

RUSSELL AND WADDELL were partners in a general store before teaming up with Majors in 1854. The company they have created will become the largest delivery business in the west.

THE DISCOVERY OF GOLD in California in 1848 brought thousands of people west. In 1850 California was admitted to the Union as the 31st state.

PLANNING for the Pony Express begins in January 1860. The entire operation is established in less than four months!

THE PONY EXPRESS began operations with 157 relay stations, located in the present-day states of Missouri, Kansas, Nebraska, Colorado, Wyoming, Utah, Nevada and California. At least 60 other locations have been identified as relay stations used in 19 months of mail service.

Signing up

You arrive at St Joseph, Missouri, on 3 April 1860, just in time to see a rider preparing for the very first westbound mail run. The rider, a young man not much older than you, is dressed in dark blue trousers and a bright red shirt. Across his saddle is draped a leather skirt with four pouches to carry the mail.

A large crowd has gathered, and they cheer loudly as the rider mounts his small California mustang and rides off in a cloud of dust.

Three thousand, two hundred kilometres (2,000 miles) to the west, another rider is preparing to leave Sacramento, California, on the first eastbound run. The Pony Express has begun operations!

ST JOSEPH, Missouri, is the starting point for the Pony Express because it is the western terminus for the railway and telegraph.

'PONY' is slang for a fast horse. The Pony Express will use several breeds of horses, all chosen for their stamina and strength.

THE PATEE HOUSE, a luxury hotel in St Joseph, Missouri, is the home office for the Pony Express.

Handy hint

If you can't get hired as a rider, consider handling stock or delivering supplies to relay stations.

MOST RECORDS claim Johnny Fry was the first westbound rider, but there are seven men who have been identified as having ridden the first leg of the inaugural trip west.

We had the pleasure of laying before the readers...news brought from the city of St Louis, across the continent, in nine days! This unparalleled feat was accomplished by the 'Pony Express'.

The San Francisco Daily Evening Bulletin
Friday, 13 April 1860

'Go west, young man!'

For the past 20 years, tens of thousands of Americans have been migrating westward across prairies, deserts and mountains in search of new opportunities in the west.

These pioneers face many challenges, but the most difficult is crossing the Rocky Mountains. The Oregon Trail follows the North Platte River valley across Nebraska and eastern Wyoming, and the Sweetwater River from Fort Caspar to South Pass. It is the easiest way to cross the Continental Divide. This route is so successful that most westward travellers use at least a portion of it, as will the railways and telegraph when they are built.

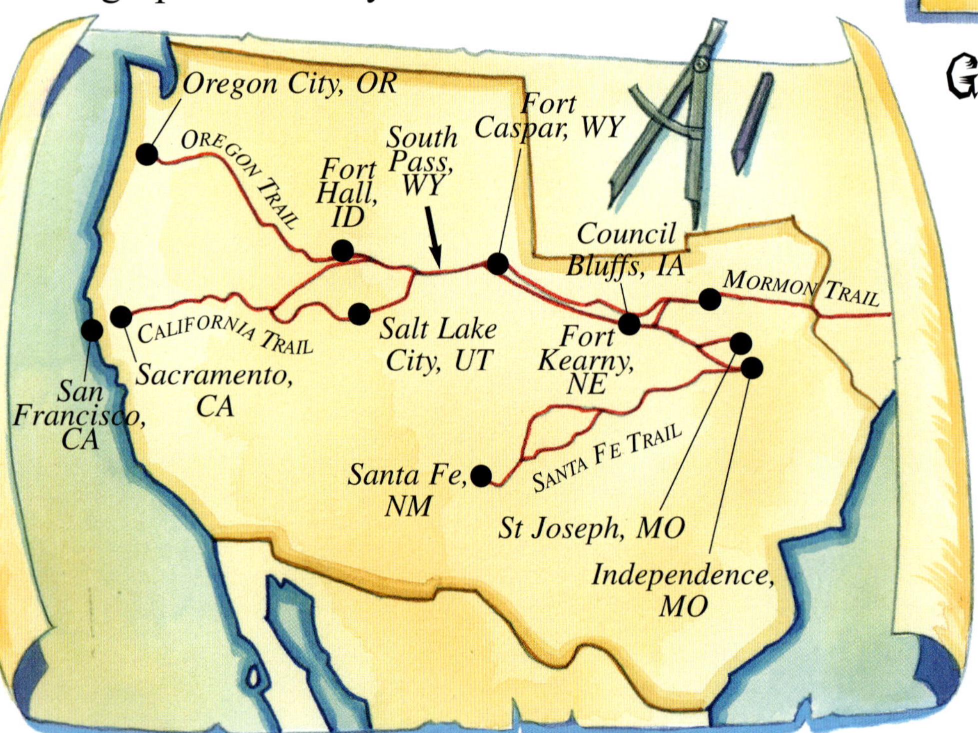

Gateway to the west

SOUTH PASS was discovered in 1812 by trader Robert Stuart. It was rediscovered and popularised in 1824 by Jedediah Smith (above), an explorer and adventurer who lived in the mountains for much of his life.

IN THE BEGINNING, Native Americans used unmapped trails before the settlers did. Although these trails were not well worn at the start, eventually the steady flow of pioneers helped to establish permanent routes such as the Oregon, California, Mormon and Santa Fe Trails.

EVERY YEAR hundreds of pioneers die en route. All who make the trip are gambling that they won't be delayed or defeated by flooded rivers, mountain snows, Indian attacks, starvation or disease.

Floods

Snow

Disease

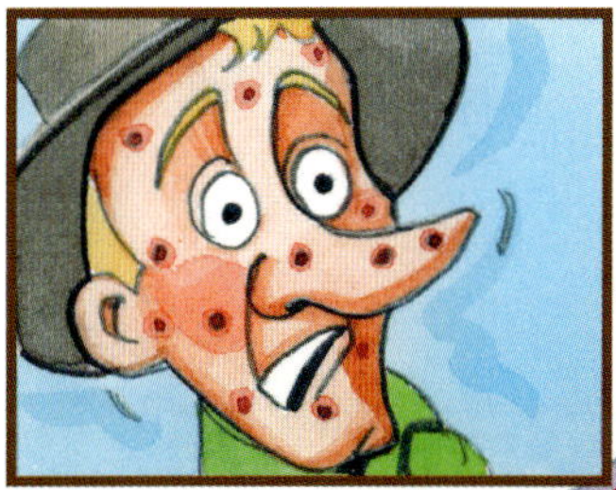

SO MANY WAGONS travel the Oregon Trail that their wheels wear permanent ruts in the prairie and even in the exposed bedrock.

The mail service

Mail service to California is slow and unreliable. Wagon trains from Fort Kearny, Nebraska, take up to six months. Clipper ships can reach San Francisco in about half that time, but they must sail around Cape Horn at the tip of South America – a trip of 29,000 km (18,000 miles). Stagecoaches are faster, but as there are no roads through the mountains, early stagecoach routes swing south through Texas, New Mexico and Arizona, adding 1,300 km (800 miles) to the trip.

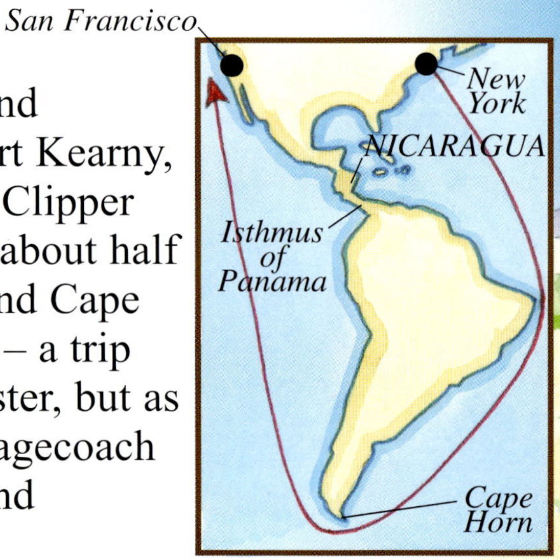

Stagecoaches take four to six weeks to cover the 4,500 km (2,800 miles) from St Louis to San Francisco.

Handy hint

If you meet up with trouble, rely on your horse's speed to outrun your attackers.

A WAGON AND FERRY SERVICE across Nicaragua in the late 1840s, and a railway line across the Isthmus of Panama in 1855, shorten the trip from New York to San Francisco by 12,700 km (7,900 miles). This cuts the mail delivery time to about 25 days.

THE BRITISH GOVERNMENT uses the Pony Express to send communications from India, China and Australia by way of San Francisco. It takes 13 days for the mail to reach New York (by pony and then railway) and another 10 to cross the Atlantic on a packet boat or steamer.

**On Her Majesty's Service (that is, on British government business).*

RIDERS who perform bravely or ride longer routes can earn a bonus of up to $50 a month. That's an extra two weeks' money!

Life on the trail

RIDERS are given Bibles and have to swear a rider's oath.

Home stations are located every three to five stops – 80 to 130 km (50 to 80 miles) or so – and provide living quarters for the riders. Smaller 'swing stations' provide fresh horses in between. Your route runs between home stations. You ride your route in one direction, get a day or two off, then make the return run.

If you reach a swing station and there is no replacement horse, you must keep going, being careful to make sure your mount does not give out before you reach the next stop. And if you reach a home station and there is no replacement rider available, you have to keep going until you are relieved.

THE RIDER'S OATH

While in the employ of A. Majors, I agree not to use profane language, get drunk, gamble, treat animals cruelly, or do anything else that is incompatible with the conduct of a gentleman.

John Smith

EACH RIDER is issued with two revolvers, a rifle and a Bowie knife, but company policy is that you should never fight unless there is no other option. A lost pistol would cost you $40.

HORSESHOES are vital to make sure company ponies remain sure-footed on the uneven terrain. The stock handler checks each horse's hooves weekly and repairs or replaces any damaged or worn shoes.

THE KEEPER of a home station (above) has to be a cook, carpenter, doctor, horse trainer, blacksmith – and even a substitute rider when needed.

You can earn extra money by running errands, taking care of horses, or helping to unload supply wagons.

SOME RIDERS routinely ride over 160 km (100 miles) at a stretch, and occasionally a man might have to cover two or three sections of a route before being relieved. The mail must go through!

The route west

The Pony Express follows the Oregon Trail as far as South Pass, then turns south through the Uinta (*yoo-EEN-ta*) Mountains to Salt Lake City. From there it follows the California Trail across the salt flats of Utah and the high desert of Nevada before crossing the Sierra Nevada mountains into California. The route is divided into five sections or divisions, each under the control of a supervisor who has to maintain the relay stations. Managing 30 or more stations over a 640 km (400-mile) stretch of wilderness is challenging – yet the mail is never delayed by a lack of supplies or horses.

RIDERS leaving St Joseph cross the Missouri River by ferryboat. In Sacramento, horse and rider board a river steamer (below) down the Sacramento River to San Francisco.

TO PROTECT and supply pioneers, a series of forts and trading posts have been built along the trails west.

A LIKELY STORY. Legend has it that the doughnut was invented by a young woman whose boyfriend rode for the Pony Express. He could catch the doughnut on his finger as he galloped past her!

The Pony Express route

FORT KEARNY in Nebraska, Forts Laramie and Caspar in Wyoming, and Fort Churchill in Nevada are key defensive points for the Pony Express.

Handy hint

Get to know the pioneer families on the trail. You can't have too many friends out here!

THE ONLY complete map of the Pony Express route was drawn by William Henry Jackson in 1866 – five years after the company shut down.

The Paiute War

Many Native Americans dislike the wagon trains and stagecoaches that cross their lands. They resent pioneers who destroy local ecosystems by overhunting, grazing cattle on scarce grasslands, and polluting rivers and streams. When the Pony Express builds relay stations across the Nevada desert, the Paiute people rebel. In early May 1860, settlers kidnap two Paiute girls, and in retaliation a small band of Indians attacks the Express station at Williams, killing five men. The company has no option but to shut down until peace is restored.

So, after only five weeks on the trail, you are out of a job!

EACH RIDER is supposed to wear a uniform consisting of blue trousers and a red shirt to make him easy to see at a distance. This is not always a good thing…

FOR THE NEXT SEVEN WEEKS there is sporadic fighting. Seven Pony Express stations are burned, 150 horses are stolen, and 16 company employees lose their lives.

THE CONFLICT ENDS when army troops and a group of California militia arrive and defeat the Paiute in a short battle. The brief war has cost Russell, Majors and Waddell about $75,000.

WHEN MAIL SERVICE starts again in late June, the Pony Express Company doubles the number of mail deliveries each week in hopes of making up some of the lost revenue.

EVEN THOUGH the Paiute War ends quickly, relations with Native American tribes remain difficult. There are several Indian nations along the trail, including the Sioux, Shoshone, Arapaho, Ute, Omaha, Pawnee and Cheyenne, as well as dozens of smaller groups.

Tools for the job

The Express Company uses special saddles made by Israel Landis of St Joseph, Missouri. He models his design on the California saddle used by Spanish *vaqueros* (cowboys). The result is a lightweight saddle, comfortable for long hours of riding.

The horses are specially chosen, too. Long-legged stallions are used for galloping over the prairies of Kansas and Nebraska, and shorter, sturdier mustangs for the rugged terrain of the mountains and deserts.

The mail is carried in a *mochila*, a leather covering that fits over the saddle and can be transferred easily from horse to horse.

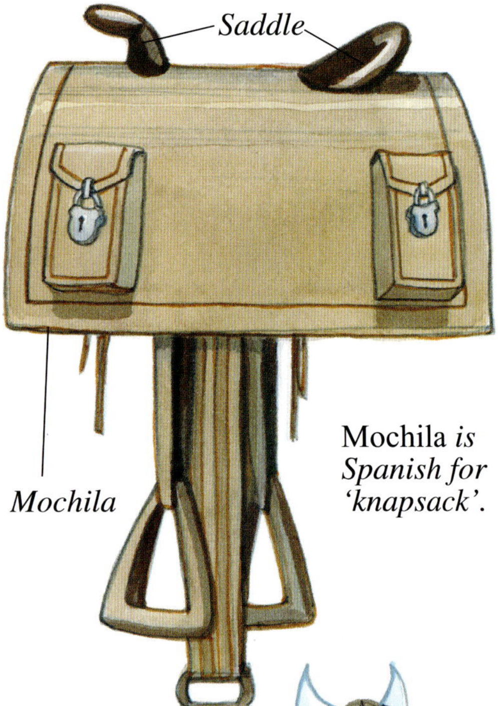

Mochila *is Spanish for 'knapsack'.*

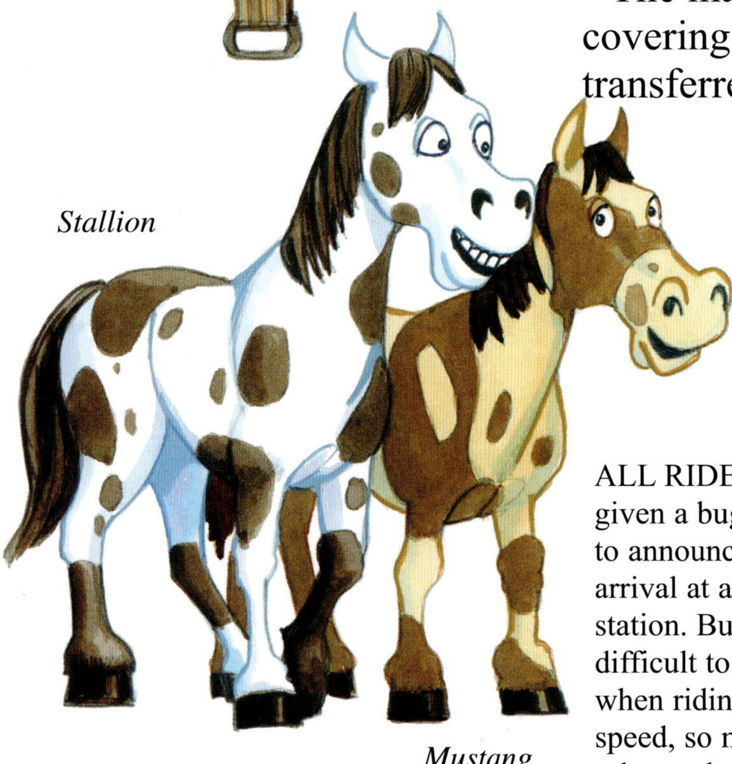

ALL RIDERS are given a bugle to blow to announce their arrival at a relay station. But it is difficult to use it when riding at full speed, so most men rely on shouting to announce themselves.

THE TOTAL WEIGHT of the saddle, bridle and mochila is 6 kg (13 lb) – about a third of the weight of the average Western saddle.

Riding over rough terrain at high speeds is tough on your body. Get plenty of food and rest on your days off.

THE MOCHILA has four small locked pouches or *cantinas*. One of these is for local mail, and the keys to this are kept at each home station. The keys to the other cantinas are kept at the terminus stations at St Joseph and Sacramento, and possibly at military outposts along the route.

The dangers of the trail

As a rider you face constant hardships: dehydration and heat exhaustion in summer; blizzards, frostbite and sub-zero temperatures in winter. Riding hard 6 to 10 hours a day is bone-jarring work and can be dangerous, especially at night. You are expected to average 16 kph (10 mph) – faster than a very fit person can run. But at times you must ride at full speed, or 32 to 39 kph (20 to 24 mph), to make up for time lost due to bad weather, accidents or floods. The pace is just as exhausting for your horse as it is for you, which is why fresh mounts are essential to maintain a reliable, speedy service.

HEAVY RAINS can cause rivers and streams to overflow their banks, making passage difficult or even impossible.

SENDING MAIL by the Pony Express is expensive: $5 for a 14 g (half-ounce) letter (about $120 or £80 in today's money). A business letter might cost as much as $30, and government dispatches often range from $200 to $300.

Handy hint

Watch out for wild animals. If your horse is spooked he may throw you.

DESPITE bad weather, outlaws and other hazards, only one rider is killed while carrying mail, and only two mail sacks are lost in 19 months of service.

EXPRESS STATIONS are often targeted by outlaw gangs. Not only are horses expensive and easy to trade, but food, ammunition and clothing are valuable on the frontier, too.

The Pony still continues his usual gallop...the first of the past week, being made in three days and twenty hours from Sacramento to this city (about seven hundred miles [1,100 km])...not very bad time, when we consider that about a quarter of the distance was galloped through snow three inches [8 cm] in depth.

The Deseret News
Salt Lake City
November 1860

The telegraph

In 1844, Samuel F. B. Morse demonstrated the first telegraph system. Using a code of electrical signals he had developed, he sent a message 56 km (35 miles) across a wire stretching from Washington, DC, to Baltimore, Maryland.

The telegraph revolutionised communication. In a few years all the major cities of the eastern United States were connected by a system that allowed information to be shared quickly. Now, as the United States expands westward, more and more people dream of connecting the nation with this new technology. In June 1860 Congress authorises construction of a telegraph line to California.

If the telegraph ever reaches the West Coast, you will most likely be out of a job. The ability to communicate in hours instead of days will surely doom the Pony Express!

Samuel Morse

MORSE CODE uses groups of short and long sounds (dots and dashes) to represent letters, numbers and punctuation. The letter *A* is dot-dash (·-); a full stop is dot-dash-dot-dash-dot-dash (·-·-·-).

THE RECEIVING OPERATOR'S telegraph key clicks out the dots and dashes, and the operator writes out the message one character at a time.

THE TRANSCONTINENTAL TELEGRAPH is built by two crews, one working east and one west. They meet at Salt Lake City.

MESSAGES sent long distances have to be copied and recopied several times, so mistakes are common.

CAN IT BE DONE? The surveyors, engineers and construction crews will have to work in the territorial lands of the various groups of Native Americans, crossing three mountain ranges, dozens of rivers and 800 km (500 miles) of desert.

The troubled election of 1860

By 1860 the nation is hopelessly divided between the 15 southern states where slavery is lawful, and the 18 northern and western states where it is forbidden. With a civil war looming, it is essential to keep the West Coast well informed of current political news.

Abraham Lincoln wants to limit the spread of slavery. When he is elected president, the southern states consider secession (leaving the Union). There are rumours that southern sympathisers might try to intercept the Express riders carrying the election results, but the news safely reaches California from Washington in 7 days and 17 hours – a record for cross-country mail.

You are proud to be a part of this historic trip. After such a performance, surely Congress will reward the Pony Express with the US Mail contract!

WITHIN A FEW MONTHS of the election seven southern states secede, forming the Confederate States of America. If President Lincoln can't persuade the states to return peacefully, the division might become permanent.

**From President Lincoln's first inaugural address, 4 March 1861*

Handy hint

The Pony Express carries vital government documents. Watch out for enemy raiders or spies.

The news of the recent Presidential election ...reached California in six days* from St Louis...we Californians are full of gratitude to its enterprising and patriotic protectors, Mssrs Russell and Majors, for the miracle they have wrought in our behalf.

The Morning Transcript
Nevada, California
19 November 1860

**The newspaper may have exaggerated the speed of the service.*

Above left: WHEN PRESIDENT LINCOLN delivers his first inaugural address, William Russell creates a special Pony Express run. He hires extra riders and provides fresh horses every 16 km (10 miles).

Above: ON 12 APRIL 1861 Confederate forces bombard Union troops in South Carolina at Fort Sumter, in Charleston harbour. The nation is at war! Now the mission of the Pony Express is more important than ever.

The end of the Express

With the nation at war, Congress must make a decision about the mail service to California. Many politicians favour stagecoaches, which can carry magazines and packages as well as letters and newspapers. So the mail contract is awarded to the Overland Stage Company (soon to be known as Wells Fargo).

Although the Pony Express is losing money, mail deliveries continue along part of the route for another eight months, bringing urgent war news to the West Coast. But in late October 1861 the transcontinental telegraph is completed and the Pony Express finally closes down.

Handy hint

Become an army scout. Scouts are paid better than soldiers and are not expected to fight in battle.

APPROXIMATELY 250 men rode for the Pony Express, carrying 35,000 letters and telegrams in 308 cross-country runs, and covering nearly 1,000,000 km (more than 600,000 miles). By the time the last mail had been delivered, the company had lost close to a million dollars and was $200,000 in debt.

LEGEND HAS IT that one of the longest non-stop rides – 518 km (322 miles) – was made by Buffalo Bill Cody. Aged 15, he rode in Wyoming from Red Buttes to Rocky Ridge and back in less than 21 hours.

William F. Cody

THE IMAGE of heroic young men racing across the dusty plains, risking life and limb to ensure the delivery of the mail, is one of the great examples of the pioneer spirit, courage and determination of a young nation.

Glossary

Blacksmith An artisan who works with iron and steel.

Bowie knife A large knife (designed by Colonel James Bowie) popular with hunters, mountain men and pioneers.

Bunkhouse Sleeping quarters at a ranch or camp.

California mustang A small, sure-footed horse favoured by cowboys.

Cantina A pouch or bag that goes over a saddle; the mail pouch in the mochila.

Civil War The four-year struggle (1861–1865) over slavery and states' rights between the United States and the Confederate States of America.

Continental Divide The line defining the highest points of the Rocky Mountains; this divides the waters that flow west from the waters that flow north or east.

Dehydration A serious medical condition caused by lack of water.

Ecosystem A community of organisms interacting with their environment.

Frostbite Skin damage caused by extreme cold.

Home station A station where riders lived when off duty. Pony Express routes ran between home stations.

Inaugural address A speech given by a new president upon being sworn into office.

Isthmus of Panama The narrowest point of Central America. An isthmus is a narrow strip of land connecting two larger landmasses.

Militia A military unit made up of private citizens from a city, region or state, who may be called upon to fight in an emergency.

Mochila The mail sack used by Pony Express riders. Its name means 'knapsack' in Spanish.

Morse code A system of short and long signals (dots and dashes) used to send messages over a telegraph line.

Packet boat A fast-sailing ship carrying passengers and mail only.

Pike's Peak A mountain in eastern Colorado.

Revenue The total money earned by a business.

Scout A person who helps pioneers or soldiers find their way on the trail or in the wilderness.

Secede To formally leave a group or nation.

Secession The act of seceding.

Slavery A system of servitude that treats people as property and forces them to work without pay or rights.

Southern sympathiser A person who agreed with southern states leaving the Union and supported slavery.

Stagecoach A four-wheeled, horse-drawn carriage used to transport passengers, luggage and mail.

Stock handler A person who takes care of horses or cattle.

Swing station A smaller station located between home stations where fresh horses were provided for riders.

Telegraph A system for sending and receiving messages over long distances, using copper wire to transmit electrical signals.

Terminus The end point of a route.

Wagon train A group of wagons travelling together, carrying passengers and supplies.

Wilderness An unsettled, wild region or territory.

Wiry Thin but strong.

Index